DOWSING

in Devon and Cornwall

Alan Neal

Bossiney Books · Launceston

Contents

Author's note

Throughout the book, in certain instances names have been changed. This has been done solely in order to protect the privacy of the individuals concerned.

First published 2001 by Bossiney Books
Langore, Launceston, Cornwall PL15 8LD
Copyright © 2001 Alan Neal
All rights reserved
ISBN 1-899383-39-5
The maps and diagrams are by Robin Paris
Printed in Great Britain by R Booth (Troutbeck Press), Mabe, Cornwall

Beginnings

One day, a long time ago, I stood on a cliff top at the western edge of Britain. It was early summer, and the air, filled with the scent of gorse blossom, was warm and still. The Atlantic, that great fearsome beast of an ocean, for once lay green and dormant before me, lapping gently at the granite far below.

Slowly I began walking forwards over the soft warm turf, my gaze fixed firmly on the piece of wire clasped in my right hand. Nothing was happening! I felt cheated and disillusioned, the sceptic in me getting ready to spring up and shout, 'I told you so!' But just then I thought I detected a vague, almost imperceptible, movement. Surely, I reasoned, I must be imagining this; or had I deliberately tilted my hand, causing the balance to alter and shift the rod's position?

I stopped, turned, and retraced my steps – but yes – this time there was no doubt. At one particular spot the wire had moved. Again and again I walked over the same piece of ground until I was finally convinced that it, or to be more precise, dowsing, far from being an elusive figment of the imagination, was a reality. I was elated. At that moment the dowsing rod was a key unlocking the gate to a whole new territory where horizon after horizon would unfold.

For most people dowsing is associated only with the search for water. This in itself is a specialised business, and many dowsers spend the whole of their working lives doing nothing else, but by using the same techniques other things can be found: minerals, buried remains of ancient buildings, underground pipes and cables, missing people – to name but a few.

In this book I shall explore some of the many uses to which dowsing can be put, visiting places throughout Devon and Cornwall which over the years I have come to know well. Each one has its own special 'feel' and entices me back time and again.

Tools of the trade

'L' rods

Worldwide, the variety of dowsing tools is enormous, probably running into hundreds of items, but the simplest, and in my opinion the most accurate, are the 'L' rods.

You can make these very easily with a length of wire, and a metal coat-hanger is excellent for the job (see fig. 1).

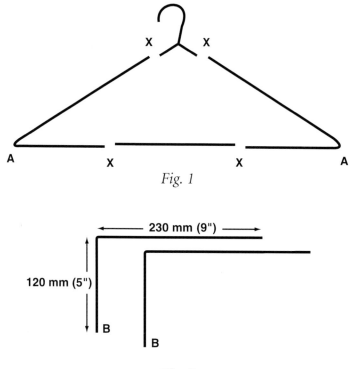

Fig. 1

Fig. 2

To save yourself extra work, use the bends (A) already in the hanger, and with a sharp pair of pliers cut where indicated at X. With a little more bending, before long you should have your dowsing rods (see fig. 2). The measurements in the diagram are those which, after a lot of trial and error, I have found give the best degree of balance and sensitivity.

4

The search position

A word of warning! The ends can be sharp and, in the hands of an over-enthusiastic beginner, dangerous. To make them safer, bend them over or bind insulating tape around them. Neither safety measure will affect the working of your rods.

In time you may find you need heavier gauge wire to counteract the effect of a strong wind, but to start with, given fair weather, your adapted coat hanger will be adequate.

Wire L rods are usually used in pairs, with the short end in the palm of the hand, but they can also be used singly. Keeping your elbows tucked into your sides, hold the rods not too tightly, with the points dipped slightly forwards, about 300 mm (12 in) apart. Aim to feel comfortable and relaxed in your body and mind.

Now decide what you are searching for, and concentrate on that one item. But don't concentrate too hard! Remember that the dowser's greatest asset is a relaxed state of mind; the greatest disadvantage is anxiety, bringing with it tension and consequent loss of accuracy.

The beginner's
'found' position

With a clear idea of the object of your search fixed in your mind, point the rods straight ahead and start walking forwards. Let's suppose you are looking for an underground watercourse, an aquifer. As you approach it, you will see the points of the rods coming together and crossing. If you are new to dowsing, this will be your 'found' position. (Later, as you progress, the rods will go past the crossover point until they are parallel to each other. This is the 'found' position for the experienced dowser.)

You are now directly above the target of your search. If you carry on walking, the rods will turn inwards towards your body. When this happens, it means you have overshot your target. Step slowly backwards until they are once again parallel.

You may find that instead of being parallel to each other in the found position, your rods turn outwards, forming a straight line. Don't panic! As individuals we all differ slightly in many ways, and this is just one of them; so for you this is 'found'.

Practise with the L rod. It is an uncomplicated and accurate tool that will help you build up confidence before you move on to other dowsing instruments, such as the V-shaped hazel rod (see page 10), which is the traditional water-finder's tool, or the pendulum (see opposite).

It is worth remembering that whatever instrument you decide to use, none of them possess any magical quality of their own, no matter what sort of material they are made of. They are nothing more than inanimate objects amplifying the reactions of your mind to objects you are seeking.

The ability to dowse is something I firmly believe is within all of us, and that as well as the five senses we use in our everyday lives we have a sixth sense, intuition. Our materialistic culture has taught us to believe only in that which can be seen, and to reject all else. I feel it is because of this misguided philosophy that intuition is so often ignored, relegated to some backwater of the mind. For too long it has remained dormant, but with dowsing it can be reawakened and brought to the fore to serve us well.

For some years now I have been running dowsing courses. Before the beginning of each one I always make a point of telling my students that I'm not going to teach them to dowse, but what I can do is to show them that they already have the innate ability to do it themselves. Once they have discovered this, we can go on together and develop what is an entirely natural and very useful art.

The pendulum

This a dowsing tool of great versatility and comes in many shapes and forms, depending on the use to which it is being put. The lightweight pointed variety is ideal for dowsing over maps; other types – small, light and often made of crystal – are employed in various forms of health dowsing such as homeopathy, healing and allergy testing.

A selection of pendulums

Heavier pendulums are best for outdoor work, as they are less likely to be affected by the wind. These sometimes have a screw-on top and a hollow interior where small samples of whatever is being sought ('witnesses') can be placed.

All sorts of material can be used for pendulums: pieces of wood or metal not originally made for the purpose, keys, wedding rings, cotton reels, nuts and bolts – anything which has sufficient weight to be suspended on a piece of string, as long as it is not too lop-sided, will suit the purpose. My first pendulum, which I still have, is a gutter bolt on a piece of twine from a turnip sack!

There are many myths about pendulums as well as a long list of supposed do's and don'ts: some materials will work better than others, wood is better than plastic, crystal is more effective than wood, metal should not be used, never use anyone else's pendulum, etc, etc. Over the years I've put many of these assertions to the test and found them to be untrue. It's really all down to personal belief – if you believe strongly enough that something will or will not work for you, then that is what will happen, but keep an open mind and all things are possible.

For everyday dowsing work the pendulum should be held on a length of string measuring about 10 cm (4 in) between the thumb and forefinger. The wrist should be slightly arched, with the elbow held against the side of the body (for map dowsing the string is kept shorter – see page 19). Just as with any other kind of dowsing, be as relaxed as possible.

When searching with a pendulum you can either hold it static or you can start it oscillating. I find the latter to be most effective, as it gives me more clear-cut and rapid results. When it is over your target, the 'found' signal will be a gyration.

Other uses of the pendulum

With a pendulum you can access your own intuition and obtain answers to questions in the form of 'yes' or 'no'. For me, 'yes' is a clockwise gyration, while 'no' is anti-clockwise. Unfortunately, this is not the same for everyone: you might get an anti-clockwise gyration for 'yes' and perhaps a clockwise one for

Holding the pendulum

'no'. And don't be surprised if none of these scenarios happens for you: a straight swing forwards and back in any direction – what I call an 'oscillation' – is also quite common.

Fortunately there is a way of determining your particular code. Set the pendulum oscillating, and ask a series of questions to which you already know the answers.

These should be simple questions which can only invoke a 'yes' or 'no' response. Repeat them several times to be sure you have consistent results.

Sometimes the reply may be neither of your usual signals, or perhaps an indeterminate mixture of the two. What this usually means is that you have asked an ambiguous question to which a straightforward 'yes' or 'no' cannot be given. The answer you're getting is something in between: a 'maybe'. When this happens, rephrase the question and try again.

The yes/no method can be used to establish the age of buildings or artifacts, and is helpful in archaeological dowsing when, for example, standing over old foundations. You can also dowse for the age of small objects by either holding them in one hand or placing them on a table in front of you.

Hold the pendulum over whatever it is you wish to date, start it oscillating, and ask (for instance): 'Is this more than 1000 years old?' If the response is 'yes', then continue by asking: 'Is it more than 2000 years old?' Now the reply may be 'no', which means you have established that it is 1000 and something years old.

To establish that 'something', set the pendulum swinging again and ask: 'Is it more than 1100 years old?', 'Is it more than 1200 years old?', and so on, until you are given a 'no' reply.

This may happen after asking: 'Is it more than 1900 years old?' and indicates that the age of the object you are dating is around 1800 years. Should you wish to be more accurate, you could then continue, starting at 1800 and counting in 10s until arriving at a final figure.

The 'V' rod

Last of all I come to the 'V' rod, a tool that has been used for centuries by generations of water finders. Traditionally it was cut from the hazel tree whose wood is pliable and retains its flexibility for a long time. Linked strongly to this custom was the belief that hazel was sacred, containing the essence of life that gave it powers beyond those possessed by other trees.

Another advantage of hazel is that it is a common hedgerow species and so is easily obtainable: even if a stick breaks, which they sometimes do, another can soon be found. However, although large rods look impressive, I have learned from experience that they are tiring to use because of the tension that needs to be maintained. And they can also be very efficient at removing skin from the palms of hands!

Despite the hazel's claim to supernatural powers, there are other woods and materials which are just as effective for use as V rods. Ash and willow twigs can work equally well, and I have seen rods fashioned from wire, plastic and nylon, the last being my favoured choice. Nylon remains flexible, will never break, and when it's over the dowsing target it will give a gentle reaction – unlike the rapid kick from a wooden rod. I purchased my nylon rod from The British Society of Dowsers, which sells a wide range of dowsing equipment (see address on page 80).

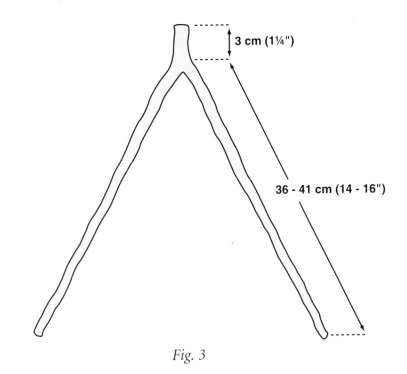

3 cm (1¼")

36 - 41 cm (14 - 16")

Fig. 3

When cutting a wooden V rod, look for the smaller, thinner sticks (although too thin a piece of wood may break straight away) growing on the outer branches of the tree. The main criterion is that both forks should be of an equal thickness. Make sure you leave around 3 cm (1¹/₄ in) of stem at the base, to avoid splitting. Each fork should be around 36-41 cm (14-16 in) long (see fig. 3).

Unlike the L rods and the pendulum, which require very little in the way of a specialised holding technique, the V rod must be held correctly for it to work. This requires creating a degree of tension so that the instrument becomes like a loaded spring which can be activated by the slightest muscular reaction: as with all dowsing instruments, it is triggered by the operator's sixth sense.

With your upper arms and elbows comfortably against the sides of your body, and your forearms outstretched, hold each fork across your upward-facing open palm.

Now bring your fingers down over the forks, pulling the forks outwards. At the same time exert a downward pressure with the

11

Holding the V rod in the search position

inner side of your hands (see photograph). It is these two actions which create the desired springy tension.

The rod can either be held parallel to the ground or, as I find preferable, at an angle of 45° to your body. You are now in the search position. Walk forwards, keeping in your mind a clear image of whatever you are seeking. When over it, your V rod will spring either upwards or downwards, both of which represent the found position – this will vary from dowser to dowser.

Although occasionally people find they can use the V rod straight away, for the majority it is not an easy tool to master. But persevere and success will eventually come.

A group of students on one of the author's courses, searching for underground water

The church of St Mary Major once stood to the west of Exeter Cathedral. Now all that remains is a cross, marking the position of the altar, mounted on what was the tip of the spire

The vanished church – dowsing with L rods

It was a Friday afternoon in February when we arrived at Exeter Cathedral Close, a haven of tranquillity in the bustle of a busy city. I say 'we' because I had with me a party of dowsing students, and our business that day was to trace the foundations of one of Exeter's vanished churches, St Mary Major. A steady sprinkling of drizzle had thinned the gathering of sightseers who normally frequent the area, leaving us to go about our business undisturbed.

I still have childhood memories of what was a typical Victorian church, complete with spire, standing not far from the west end of the cathedral. Ornately respectable yet giving the impression of having seen better days, it was constructed between 1865 and 1868, and occupied the site of a much earlier medieval church of the same name. It was deemed surplus to church requirements and demolished in 1971.

With dowsing, as well as being able to find where hidden objects are now, we can also reveal where they used to be.

Nobody has been able to give a scientific explanation for this, but I am convinced that our sixth sense plays a major part.

Asking the question 'Where are the foundations?', and holding my rods in the search position, I moved to the east of the cross. Almost immediately the tips started to come together, finishing up parallel to each other. Here then was the line of the east wall. Turning to my left so that I was now facing north, I began walking with the rods once more at 'search'. A little further on and they swung sharply to the left. I had reached the corner of the building and now began following the north wall. Eventually the whole outline of the church had been traced: the base of the spire with its west door, the positions of the larger windows, the nave, and the outline of the altar.

Although we had found the whereabouts of all these features, it is doubtful if any tangible evidence remains even below the ground surface. After the demolition of St Mary Major, much of this area was excavated by archaeologists who subsequently revealed the baths of the Roman town of *Isca Dumnoniorum*. The baths were left intact but reburied and any remains in the soil above them would have been destroyed during the dig.

Although the rain had driven away the usual flock of curious onlookers who gather on these occasions, we were not totally alone. As we carried on our work, I became aware of the faint metallic chatter of a radio, and noticed that from the nearby path two traffic wardens were watching us. By the look on their faces I could tell they were fascinated, if not a little mystified, by our antics. One of them, it transpired, had seen dowsing used successfully to find water; the other was interested but sceptical.

I searched around for the nearest line of underground water, and after a quick lesson in the correct way to hold L rods, let the wardens try for themselves. At first, as is common, the rod movements were only slight, but then much to their delight their technique began to improve. My one lasting memory of that afternoon is of two traffic wardens marching side by side in the drizzle, in the shadow of the great cathedral, radios chattering and dowsing rods swinging happily in unison.

Angela Evans, owner of Pengersick Castle, is one of those people who exudes such optimistic enthusiasm that it becomes infectious, especially where the castle is concerned.

Her knowledge of every facet of its history is encyclopaedic, from its beginnings in the twelfth century right up to the present day

'Circle of search' at Pengersick Castle

Mention the name Pengersick to most people and the chances are you'll be met with a mystified expression; but speak of Praa Sands and you're more likely to prompt fond memories of a sandy beach, caravan park, putting green, fish and chips, ice cream and all the familiar paraphernalia of a seaside holiday. But most of this scenario only arrived within the last hundred years. Before then the picture would have been very different: no bungalows, no cafe or car parks or caravans – just a long sandy beach flanked by dunes. Behind would have been marsh-land, then farms, cottages and a castle.

Approaching Praa Sands (pronounced 'Pray' and not as so

many insist 'Prah') from Germoe Cross on the A394, the road runs past a golf course and modern bungalows before descending steeply through woodland. It is surprising to see that some of the original granite cottages still remain here, unmolested by developers. Even more startling is the first glimpse of the castle: with its mullioned windows and neat castellations it looks too perfect to be real, but real it most certainly is, with a history to match any fictional castle.

Over the years I had driven past many times, but it wasn't until 1995 that I made my first visit when the owner, Angela Evans, held an open day. The first early medieval mansion was built on a plateau on what is now a wooded hillside. It is some distance from the subsequent fortified late medieval manor which was built around the second half of the fifteenth century by the Pengersick family. Largely by a succession of well-planned marriages, they had become wealthy and so were able to construct a new, grander dwelling.

The castle's history, riddled with violence and intrigue, borders on the brink of legend. Here are all the best ingredients – murder, magic, wrecking, hauntings – for a gothic novel begging to be written. Since that memorable first visit, time and again I have felt drawn back to Pengersick. There is so much waiting to be revealed, so many plots to unravel. In short, it is a dowser's paradise…

It was while walking around the medieval herb garden that my interests were first aroused. The guide spoke of the site of the old family chapel being somewhere nearby – but where? All she could say was that it was possibly in the vicinity of the garden. I quickly went and fetched the pair of L rods that, together with a compass, go everywhere with me in the car, and began searching, watched by a large audience of other visitors.

The technique I used was one called the 'circle of search'. This involves standing in one spot, rods in the search position, and slowly pivoting until they cross at an angle of 90°. When this happens, stop and take a sighting through the centre of that angle (see photograph). Somewhere in a direct line with that sighting will be the object you seek.

The 'found' position for the circle of search

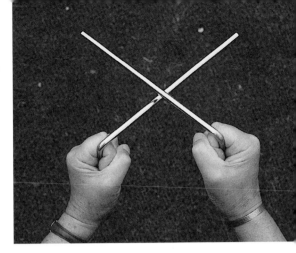

On this occasion, as I pivoted I kept the question 'Where is the chapel?' clearly in my mind. Having taken my sighting, I walked forwards, searching, and when the rods came together in the parallel found position, I stopped. Directly beneath the rods was the edge of a wall. I placed a large stone on the spot, and began following the perimeter of the building, placing more stones or pieces of wood as markers as I went along.

When dowsing, I become so involved with the job in hand that I lose all sense of time, but I suppose the whole operation must have taken between half and three quarters of an hour, at the end of which I had the very definite rectangular shape of a building. A compass bearing taken along one of the longer sides showed an east–west orientation, a good indicator that this could indeed have been a church. (There are other clues which can be revealed by dowsing to show whether or not a building was a church. These involve earth energy and water – see page 47.)

Before leaving, I was able to obtain some pieces of batten which I hammered into the ground as more permanent markers. Many an hour of painstaking work has been lost through inadequate marking!

The most frustrating part of archaeological dowsing can be the long wait for confirmation of results. Although I know what I've found – in this case it was building foundations – it is very difficult convincing anyone else unless real proof can be viewed.

Some time later, an encouraging piece of evidence emerged. A geophysical survey was carried out on the site which revealed what looked very like the outline of a building. But to many people seeing is believing: a real wall rather than just a shadow image on paper was called for.

The wait was lengthy. Four years later, in the autumn of 1999, I received a phone call from an excited Angela. While reconstructing a boundary wall to the herb garden, foundations had been revealed. After a little more investigation, it became obvious that directly beneath the pegs I had knocked in the ground there really was the outline of a building. Here at last was indisputable evidence. The long wait had been worthwhile.

Map dowsing with a pendulum

One aspect of dowsing that above all else evokes the critical protests of sceptics is the use of maps, diagrams and photographs to establish the whereabouts of whatever we may be seeking. Finding things in the ground whilst walking on an area of the earth's surface does have a probable scientific explanation. The planet, with its core of molten metals, radiates its own magnetic field which humans have lived with and grown accustomed to over the millennia. It is anomalies in this magnetic field which dowsers detect through their instruments – anomalies caused, for instance, by subterranean water or minerals.

But all of these can, with practice, be revealed on a map just as easily as on the ground. Here attempts at an explanation start to fly rapidly out of the window, propelled by a cold draught that brings discomfort to many scientists. To find an answer, we have to look beyond the narrow parameters of present knowledge and accept that there is more to our world than can be seen with the naked eye.

In map dowsing we are calling upon the assistance of our inner vision, or some might call it their third eye, their sixth sense or their intuition. The principles of searching on a map with a pendulum are the same as those applied to any other form of dowsing: seek and it shall be revealed – if it's there!

The author map dowsing

Map dowsing for linear features

Let's take for example the search for an aquifer running beneath a field. First, you will need a map of that field, large enough to fill a sheet of A4 paper. You may have to draw this yourself. If you do, then make sure it's as accurate as possible. Sit comfortably at a table with the map in front of you. Hold the pendulum in your right or left hand (depending on whether you are right- or left-handed) on about 6 cm (2¹/₂ in) of string. In your other hand hold a pencil, the tip poised just above the surface of the paper.

Holding the pendulum alongside the top right- or left-hand corner of the map, set it into an oscillating motion. Slowly move the pencil along the top edge, asking the question: 'Where is the aquifer?' As the tip approaches water, the oscillations will begin to speed up. Then, when the pencil is directly over it, the pendulum will start to gyrate. Mark this spot with a cross, and continue searching until you have reached the opposite corner

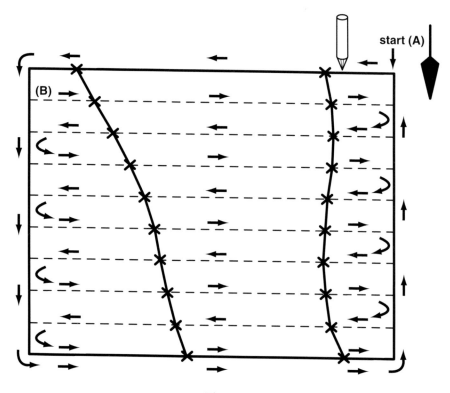

Fig. 4

of the map. Draw in more crosses wherever you obtain a similar reaction.

Continue dowsing down the opposite side of the map, along the bottom and up the other side, until you have reached the point where you started (A). Mark with a cross wherever you get a pendulum gyration (the pendulum can, if desired, be moved closer to the pencil at any time).

Returning to one of the top corners, lower the pencil down the side by approximately 2.5 cm (1 in) and work your way back across the map (B), marking crosses at reaction points. Each time the edge is reached, drop the pencil down another 2.5 cm, keeping the pendulum positioned not too far away so that you are working comfortably. Repeat the process until you have reached the bottom.

Depending on how many aquifers you've found, your map should now have one or more lines of crosses running over its surface (see fig. 4). It should be possible to join these up, so that each aquifer is clearly defined. But before beginning, it's worth making a final check. Hold the pendulum over each line of crosses in turn and start it oscillating. Then carefully move it forwards in the direction you estimate the line to be running. You will find that each forward swing will take it along the correct course. Should the direction unexpectedly alter (as it sometimes can), allow the pendulum to guide you along the right track. Remember it is your own intuition that you are really following – trust it!

Now go to the area with your rods, and dowse on foot over the ground. First, work around the perimeter, then traverse the field several times, marking each reaction point with a peg. The final result may not exactly tally with your map the first time, but with a little practice accuracy will improve.

In this instance I have used an aquifer as an example, but the same technique can be used for tracing lost tracks or footpaths or, on a larger scale map, the foundations of buildings.

Single object dowsing

So far we've looked at tracing something that runs across a map in a line, but there are times when it's necessary to search for a single object, perhaps a long forgotten well, or the original position of a wayside cross that has been moved, or it could be you want to find the whereabouts of a lost or stolen item.

You will need a good map of the area in question. I find the Ordnance Survey 1:50,000 (1¼ inches to 1 mile) ideal for the purpose. Either the whole map can be dowsed or, if needs be, it can be divided into smaller sections. The grid reference lines can be used as boundaries.

With the map laid out in front of you, follow the same procedure as before – pendulum oscillating at the top right- or left-hand corner, pencil or pointer held in the other hand. Ask the question: 'Where is - - - ?'

Now move the pointer across the top of the map. If the object of your search is in the area covered, at some stage the pendulum will begin to oscillate faster and then gyrate. Mark the spot your pointer is over when this happens. The cross you have just pencilled in will now be directly above and in line with whatever it is you are looking for. To pinpoint its exact location, you now have two alternatives:

(a) Set the pendulum oscillating, and follow the vertical line down from your cross at the top of the map until it begins to gyrate.

(b) Start the pendulum oscillating roughly half way across the map and slowly move your pointer down along one side, starting at the top right- or left-hand corner. Mark its position when the pendulum starts to gyrate. Draw a horizontal line into the map, at 90° to the edge. The object of your search should be where vertical and horizontal lines converge (see fig. 5).

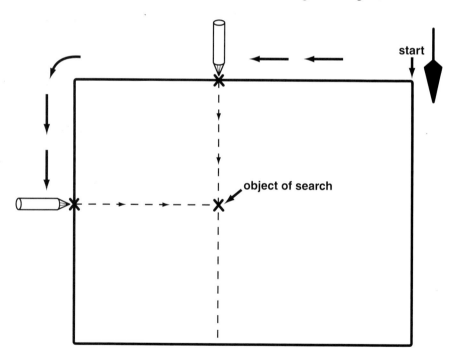

Fig. 5

Dowsing and healing

Discovering that there is a connection between dowsing and healing comes as a surprise to many people, but the principles employed in the quest for water can be applied equally well to the living body to search out and correct problems. It is a subject of great diversity, already filling scores of volumes, and ranges far beyond the confines of this book, so here I will give just a brief summary.

To maintain a healthy existence all living beings depend on a state of balance and harmony both within themselves and with their surroundings. This balance can sometimes, for many reasons, become disrupted, causing illness to set in. By employing certain techniques involving thought direction and concentration, the dowser can pinpoint the place where the problem originates and, wherever possible, restore a state of equilibrium. Only when this condition prevails can the body begin to heal itself.

Every animate and inanimate entity has a solid material body surrounded by an energy field, the aura, which to most people is invisible. However, it can be detected by corona discharge, or Kirlian, photography, and by dowsing. The distance of the aura from the body's surface depends on the state of health of the whole being. In most people the aura, which consists of several layers, extends out about a metre. (To give you an idea, raise and stretch out an arm to the side: the distance between your finger tips and your body is a rough guide to how large your aura is likely to be.)

A wide aura is a sign of good health, whereas a narrow one is a signal that something is wrong.

Healing a trapped nerve

Paul, like myself, is involved in adult education. He attended one of my courses in Plymouth and, after I'd given a talk on dowsing and healing, asked if there was anything that could be done to relieve the pain from a trapped nerve in his shoulder. He had sustained the injury after falling from his loft and it had been giving him a great deal of discomfort for a long time. Pain killers were only allowing temporary relief. I said I would do what I could for him, but could make no definite promise of a long-term cure. (It is always better to be fair and honest about this right from the start, rather than raising what could be false hopes. There are times when, for no accountable reason, healing just will not work.)

A couple of days later, Paul and his wife arrived at my house. I sat him down in an upright chair in front of me, and moved my left hand over his shoulder where he had indicated the pain to be, about a couple of centimetres from the body surface. I knew when I was over the exact spot: the discomfort he was feeling transferred itself to me in the form of an unpleasant throbbing, similar to that experienced when standing over a stressful underground watercourse. Meanwhile, the pendulum, held in my right hand, started gyrating in an anti-clockwise direction.

Using the pendulum as a gauge, I began drawing off negative energy from the painful area. The gyrations changed from anti-clockwise to clockwise, gradually slowing down and coming to a stop. Then I concentrated on replacing the negative energy with positive energy, drawing it in from around me and directing it into that same spot. Again, the pendulum gyrated, first anti-clockwise, then clockwise, before stopping once more.

'How does it feel now, Paul?' I asked.

He lifted his elbow and gave the offending shoulder a tentative trial shrug.

'I think it feels a bit looser.'

'Well, see how it goes and let me know in a day or two.'

They thanked me and left, and as I watched them walk down the path I thought that Paul's walk was more relaxed than before. But, as is so often the case, only time tells whether the effects of healing are long lasting.

Several days later, he rang to inform me he'd had no more pain.

'Wonderful!' I said, 'But take it easy for a while.'

All this happened about two years ago, since when I haven't seen Paul, although quite recently I happened to bump into a mutual acquaintance. During the conversation he mentioned meeting him recently and I asked how he was.

'Oh, Paul's fine. He's still running his classes, and his shoulder has given him no more trouble!'

So often there is no feedback after healing, but when it does come, however long afterwards, it makes me realise that this is the most satisfying aspect of dowsing.

Dowsing a stressful house

One morning I had a telephone call from Diane. When I'd last seen her she had told me that, since moving to her present home, an old farmhouse in mid-Devon, she'd had numerous health problems, including a recently discovered heart complaint. All this would have slowed down most other people, but not Diane. As well as travelling long distances in her work as a representative for an agricultural company, she runs her own franchise business from home, a home shared with a couple of lively dogs who need regular exercise. Normally a cheerful person, seemingly untroubled by anything life throws at her, this time there was a note of anxiety in her voice.

She asked if I could have a look at the ground plan of her house and see if there was anything that could be making her feel generally unwell. In recent weeks, as if she hadn't had enough to put up with already, she'd been confined to the house after undergoing a leg operation. It was in the two rooms where over this period she had been spending most of her time that she sensed something was wrong; she'd had an inexplicable feeling of agitation and restlessness. I asked her to send me the plan, and this arrived in the next morning's post.

With the idea of 'stress' fixed in my mind, I dowsed the perimeter of the house, with the map laid out on the table in front of me, pendulum in my right hand and pencil in my left. Stress, or to give it its full name, geopathic stress, is a condition which can be triggered by a number of circumstances, some natural, some created by humans.

As a natural condition it can be found above aquifers, particularly the stronger ones. When travelling beneath the earth's

Lydford Castle, on the western edge of Dartmoor, has a grim and brooding atmosphere. Many have perished in its dark dungeons and a strong line of geopathic stress runs through it

surface, water generates its own electromagnetic field, and this disrupts the natural radiations (ones we can happily live with) that are continually being given off by the earth. If we spend prolonged periods above places where this disruption occurs, we can become ill. Beginning with relatively minor complaints, such as sleeplessness or irritability, more serious conditions can in time develop, such as arthritis, stomach ulcers and heart trouble. It is also thought that geopathic stress could be a major culprit in triggering ME as well as some forms of cancer.

In addition to underground water courses, there are other natural sources of stress: large mineral deposits, volcanic fault lines and cave systems. Geopathic stress can also attach itself to lines of earth energy, thereby 'souring' them.

Man-made stress can originate from activities such as road making, quarrying, mining, the erection of large high buildings

– anything in fact which involves a major disturbance of the earth's surface. But we are not alone in suffering from this phenomenon. Plants, for instance, can succumb to its ill effects, and the seeds of many trees will seldom germinate over areas of stress. If they do, they develop into sickly specimens, often with twisted trunks and covered with cankerous growths. Adversely affecting most living species, geopathic stress is a very real and insidious threat, and should not be treated lightly.

As I searched the perimeter of the map there was a positive reaction in four places, two along the top and two at the base. Then, working my way backwards and forwards across its surface, travelling from top to bottom, I was able to plot the course of two lines. Diane's intuitive feelings had been correct: these two lines crossed directly beneath the rooms where she had recently been convalescing – her office and, on the floor above, her bedroom.

Using my pendulum and a pencil as a pointer, I traced each line until it was well clear of the house. Then, as accurately as I could, I marked their centres. Placing the point of the pencil directly over each one in turn, I concentrated on dispersing the stress, literally telling it to go. Just as in the trapped nerve case, I used the pendulum as a gauge, watching it first gyrating anti-clockwise, then oscillating backwards and forwards, and finally gyrating clockwise before slowing down to a stop. Lastly, I checked around the perimeter once more. There was no sign of stress. The two lines that had carried it now only reacted to requests for water and energy respectively, their original designations.

I picked up the telephone and rang Diane: 'Have a look around the house and see how it feels now – call me back later on.'

This was at around eleven o'clock in the morning, but it was not until just after one in the afternoon that she returned my call. 'I looked around once and everything seemed fine – much better. Then after lunch I thought I'd check again before phoning. Now there seems to be one place that still doesn't feel quite right.' She indicated the location on the map, and I scanned over it again. The stress had indeed returned to one line, the water line. Further action was needed.

Placing the pencil point once more on the centre of the offending aquifer, well clear of the back of the house, I drew in a new line that continued in a loop around the side wall and joined up again with its original course just outside the front garden. I had drawn in a diversion and, as I drew, I pictured in my mind's eye the stressful energy travelling along the new course away from the building, where it would do no harm.

Diane called the next morning to tell me the whole house seemed much better, with no feeling of stress anywhere. On the map, too, I could detect none within the building, but along the line's new course it was flowing as strongly as ever.

Since that day, just as in all similar cases, I've checked the ground plan of Diane's house on a weekly basis. Nothing ominous has, I'm glad to say, reappeared; but I'll keep watching just the same!

Healing an almond tree

High on a ridge below which the River Torridge winds its way through lush meadows and woodland towards Bideford and the sea stands the village of Beaford. Close by the church and just before the land drops down steeply is a large rambling house surrounded by gardens. This is the Beaford Centre.

It was early May, and for the time of year quite unusually hot, when I stayed there with a group of students on a weekend residential course. We were taking full advantage of the good weather, getting out into the gardens as much as possible for practical work.

I first noticed the almond tree when we were dowsing in the old kitchen garden for the depth of a beautifully constructed Victorian well. Not far away from where we were standing and partly hidden by a hedge, a flash of brilliant pink caught my eye. Its vividness and clarity so arrested my attention that I felt compelled to go over and have a closer look.

As I approached I realised that, although the blossom was still a vibrant colour, it was long past its prime – almond flowers are normally at their best in March or April. But now I was also noticing something else: the tree, while mature in years, was stunted; its bark was calloused and gnarled, and the tips of some of its branches were dying. Could it be, I wondered, that it was growing over the crossing point of two aquifers?

This can often be the cause of such symptoms in trees. I searched, but could find none. Clearly though, this particular almond tree was ill and, like all living things overcome with sickness, needed help.

With my left hand outstretched and my pendulum swinging in the search position in my right hand, I walked slowly towards the tree. The aura, when my fingertips found it, was just over 30 cm (12 in) from the nearest adjacent branch. For a tree of this size, small though it was, I would have expected a much wider aura. Keeping my hand at its edge, I applied the same energy balancing technique as is used on any living body. Then, stepping back from the tree, I approached it again with my left arm outstretched. The aura had widened, and was now closer to 46 cm (18 in).

The following day, I got up early. As I entered the garden, morning mist was still rising from the ground and the sky was cloudless: promises of another fine day. Once more I checked the aura of the almond tree. Its width was still the same as when I had left it the previous day.

In all, over the two-day stay at Beaford, I gave healing to the tree three times. When we came to leave, its aura measured a much healthier 90 cm (36 in). Since then I have not returned, but I believe those few minutes were well spent, however temporary any respite might have been.

Ley lines

A quick glance at a map reveals a great many features: the road system, railways, rivers, contour lines indicating the shape and height of hills, areas of woodland, houses, towns and villages. But if you take the time to look closer you can discover much more, for not only do maps represent the area as it is now, but they are also a record of its history. They show us places that

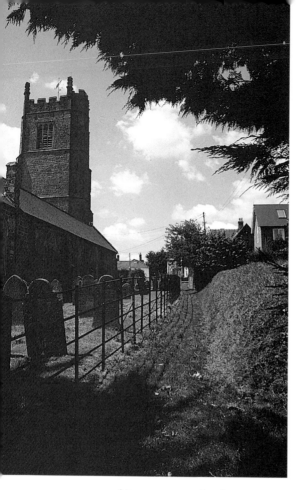

A straight pathway running behind the ancient church at Colebrook, near Crediton, follows the course of a ley line. West of here the line passes through a sacred spring and the sites of two sacred groves (nymets), before going on to North Tawton Church

were of importance in the past: castles, hill forts, Roman villas, burial mounds, stone rows and circles, crosses, ancient trackways, holy wells, ancient churches, moated manor houses...

What is their significance to us today? They are of course of great interest to the archaeologist and historian, but viewed in another way they can provide clues pointing to the existence of an intriguing enigma: the Ley System.

Find a historically significant site on your map – perhaps a pre-Reformation church or a Bronze Age stone circle. Using a ruler, try aligning it with other historic or prehistoric sites. Look for some of those mentioned above; look too for bridging points and fords on rivers, the highest spots on hills, sections of dead-straight roads and cross roads.

Names are also important, and those frequently found on ley lines are: Merry, Dod, Toot, Tot or Tut, Tump, Moot, Cole, Cold, Tan or St Anne, Bury, Burgh, Ash, Brent and Beacon, as well as Ley in its various forms, such as Lay, Lea, Leigh and Lee. In mid-Devon, Nymet will be found. This is a Celtic word meaning 'sanctuary' or 'sacred grove' and places bearing the name are always on or near a ley line.

Other names to keep an eye out for are those of colours: Red, White, Blanche, Black, Gold, or Golden. When looking at churches, wherever possible try to find out to which saint they have been dedicated. Significant names are: St Michael, St George, St Mary, St Catherine, and St Margaret, Christian saints whose attributes correspond with those of the earlier pagan deities they superseded.

If you can align five or more of these sites along a forty kilometre (twenty-five mile) stretch, this is considered more than mere coincidence, and the chances are you have found a ley line: a completely straight alignment of ancient places of importance across the landscape.

Leys vary in length from a few kilometres to considerable distances. Their very straightness leads me to believe they are man-made, but the reason for their construction is something which no one can explain with any certainty. Of all those I have found, there does seem to be one common characteristic: they can be detected by dowsing, both on the map and at ground level. It is dowsing on the ground which gives us final proof that what we have found is a true ley line.

For a detailed study of leys and everything involved in searching for them, I strongly recommend *The Old Straight Track* by Alfred Watkins. Although published in 1925 it is still in print. It is neither dated nor dry but is as fresh, readable and relevant today as when it was written. It was in this book that I first came across the information about place and colour names. Since then I've often put it to the test, and have proved time and again that Watkins was absolutely right.

Alfred Watkins had many varied interests. He was a brewer and grain merchant as well as a keen amateur photographer and naturalist. He was also an inventor, developing and manufacturing the first light meter which enabled photographers to set the apertures accurately on their cameras, thereby eliminating guesswork. It was he who rediscovered this system of ancient site alignment and gave it the name 'ley', an obsolete word for a forest glade, clearing, or enclosed pasture, because in its many forms it so frequently appears on alignments.

Having found a ley line on a map, the next step is to go out and search for it on the ground. Obviously to follow its complete course would be impracticable, unless it runs all the way through common land. But a study of your map will reveal places where it is crossed by roads, and it is here that, especially if the area is rural, checks can be carried out.

Stop in the place you estimate the line to be, and start searching with the dowsing rods. Also remember to look through gateways and where possible over hedges. Remote areas can be full of surprises: features which have escaped the attention of the map maker, such as small ponds (often found on leys), and – particularly in the low light of early morning or evening which throws even the smallest features into relief – the outline of long abandoned roads running across fields.

It is a good idea to give each ley line its own identification tag, a name, or even a number; something which your mind can latch onto. If you believe you are in the correct area, think to yourself, for example, before dowsing, 'I want to find the Blue line'. If it is there, then your dowsing instrument will react; there will be no identifiable reaction if you are in the wrong place.

And finally, if you do feel the need to go onto private land, please respect the owner's rights and always ask their permission first. It's agreeably surprising to find how often landowners will not only allow you in, but will show a genuine interest in what you are doing.

Woodbury Castle

Travelling in a north-easterly direction from Exmouth, the road climbs steadily through a tree-lined landscape before emerging on the open heath of Woodbury Common. To the west is a panoramic view of the Exe estuary, backed by a distant outline of Dartmoor tors. Ahead, at the very peak of the hill and dominating the skyline with its presence, lies Woodbury Castle, hiding beneath a dark umbrella of trees.

Different in every way from the type of stone-built structure with dungeons and drawbridge set up by the Normans, this is a castle of a much earlier kind: an Iron Age hillfort. Constructed of high earth ramparts that were topped with palisades interspersed with deep ditches, this would have been a safe haven for both people and livestock when threatened with attack.

It was built some time between 600 and 100 BC by members of the Dumnonii, a tribe occupying most of what is now Devon and Cornwall. These people spoke a Celtic language similar to today's surviving Welsh and Gaelic, and they were cultured yet capable of being fierce and war-like. They were also farmers, keeping cattle, pigs and sheep; they were able to use the plough and grow crops, mainly barley and wheat; they were skilled weavers of wool, using natural dyes to colour the cloth they produced; they could work tin and bronze, and they could make fine pottery; but most important of all they knew how to produce iron for ornaments, household and farm tools, and swords and spears for battle.

Here then was the hub of the Iron Age equivalent of a large country estate, ruled over by a warrior aristocrat or minor chieftain. In the surrounding area would have been farms, some worked by freemen, others by bondmen or estate servants. Last in the hierarchical order would have been the slaves, the general labourers. The farmers would pay tribute in the form of produce to the lord, and in return he would offer them protection within his fortifications in times of danger.

Approaching Woodbury Castle on a sunny summer's day along the footpath canopied by trees is like entering a world of

mysterious twilight, not quite belonging to the modern age. Even the noise of traffic passing on the busy nearby road is muffled as if left behind in some other dimension. It was on just such a day, not long ago, that I arrived at the edge of the first fortifications. Although eroded by both weather and the feet of visitors, the ramparts and ditches are still formidably steep, forming a treacherous barrier to the unwary.

Carefully picking my way along a well-trodden track I finally reached the rim of the inner area. Below me lay 2 hectares (5 acres) of flat ground, dotted with oak and beech trees interspersed with thick clumps of holly. It is hard to imagine this was once a bustling hive of activity filled with people and animals, and the circular huts in which they lived. No trace remains on the ground to give any hint of their presence, except for the surrounding banks and ditches.

The hut circle

Standing on the rim of the central enclosure, with rods in the search position, I pivoted around in a semi-circle, mentally asking the question: 'Where is the nearest hut circle?' It was not long before the rods started to cross. When they formed a 90° angle, I took a sighting through the angle, and walked forwards (see page 16).

I had taken no more than a dozen paces when they came together in the found position. Here was the outer edge of a wall. I turned and followed it around, letting the rods guide my direction and stopping at intervals to push a peg in the ground to mark where I'd been. I finally arrived back at the point from where I'd started.

I stepped back to obtain an overall view. The outline traced by the pegs was not quite a perfect circle and had a diameter of nearly 5 metres (16 ft). Once more I paced the perimeter, this time searching for the position of the entrance, and pegged the two places where the rods crossed. It was around 1m (3¹/₄ft) wide, and faced east-south-east. Standing within the circle, I took my pendulum from my pocket and, setting it into motion, asked: 'Was this a human habitation?'

A hut circle marked out with pegs and tape, its shape revealed by dowsing

It immediately gyrated in a wide clockwise swing: a very definite 'yes'. It was strange to think that this deserted spot on which I stood was once home to at least one, and very probably several, generations of people. Here they would have been born, and never having the need to stray more than a short distance would have spent a whole lifetime. This small area was their entire world – a hard concept for today's seasoned travellers to grasp.

A line of investigation I often follow in such places is to literally put myself in the footsteps of people of another age, following their everyday movements. First it is necessary to choose a suitable year well within the time frame of the structure in question to 'latch onto'. The Iron Age, during which the earth ramparts of Woodbury were constructed, covered a period beginning around 600 BC and continuing in many remoter places right on into the Roman occupation, its traditions and way of life little changed by Mediterranean influences.

Moving a short distance from the circle, I asked to be taken inside in the year 200 BC. As the rods turned, I allowed them, or rather my intuition, to direct my steps. The first thing I noticed was that instead of being able to walk straight in I had to turn right as soon as I had entered the doorway. A turn to the left then gave me access to the living area.

Later, more detailed dowsing revealed a wall built just inside the entrance – a good practical way of excluding draughts as well as slowing down the progress of unwanted visitors. I have never noticed this feature in reconstructed Iron Age dwellings – could it be, I wonder, something no one else has yet discovered? Further questions revealed the whereabouts of the fire, the sleeping and storage areas: the outlines of all of these could be traced by dowsing.

The well

I was aware from historical maps of the existence of 'Soldier's Well', a well below Cross Ridge dyke to the north-east of the castle (see fig. 6), but I wanted to know if there had ever been another source of drinking water nearer to the central enclosure. In the event of a siege this surely would have been vital.

Standing over the place where the fire had once been, I asked: 'Where did this family go to fetch water?' Soon I was being led back through the door, once more avoiding the 'draught excluder' wall. Then turning sharply to the left, I made my way across the central enclosure. At first it was puzzling to find that I had to make frequent sudden turns, although the general course of the route obviously led in one definite direction. Subsequent investigation revealed the reason: at each place where this happened there had been a building directly ahead, making a change of course necessary. As well as prehistoric barriers barring my progress, there were more modern ones: large trees, holly bushes and bramble thickets all had to be circumnavigated and the path retraced on the other side. So although the total distance covered could not have been more than 180 m (200 yards), it seemed much further.

A gentle pulling sensation on the palms of my hands told me

that the ends of the rods were about to cross: I was approaching the end of my search. Where they turned to the parallel found position, I drove a peg into the ground.

On initial inspection the place seemed unlikely for the site of a well. The ground was flat, as though it had never been disturbed, but I knew from past experience that appearances can be deceptive. Since the Iron Age the fort has been reused on more than one occasion. In 1549, during the Prayer Book Rebellion in the reign of Edward VI, a battle was fought here between the rebels and the forces of the king. Between 1798 and 1803, when there were threats of Napoleonic invasion, it was used as a military camp, and later in the nineteenth century it was the venue for annual army exercises.

Over the years the area has been disturbed constantly, and each autumn a carpet of fallen leaves has covered the ground, filling cavities and depressions, and eventually rotting down to soil.

Although the strongest evidence for the existence of an object below ground level comes from digging down to it, this is not always possible, and certainly not if a site is protected. But where wells are concerned, there is another option.

Throughout history and prehistory people have dowsed for water and this has enabled them, whenever possible, to obtain their supplies at the point where two aquifers cross. This is known as a blind spring, knot or spiral. At Woodbury Castle I knew that if the peg I had put in the ground was at the exact centre of one of these crossings, and providing the water was close enough to the surface to have been reached by people with limited resources, then this would be very strong evidence that I had indeed found the site of a well.

I walked about 2 metres (6^1/$_2$ ft) away from the peg and paced around it in a circle, searching for aquifers. There were two, and they crossed directly beneath it. Now I needed to find the depth of each one, and this proved to be 3.5 and 2.5m (12 and 8^1/$_4$ ft) respectively. Allowing for a build up of the ground level in the intervening years, a supply of water from this particular spot would have been easily accessible to the inhabitants of

Woodbury Castle 2000 years ago. I am convinced that, in addition to the existing well outside the ramparts, this was their second supply of water.

Ley lines

So far I have described only the Iron Age features of Woodbury that are contained within the castle; but what of the hilltop itself and the surrounding area? On my first visit, when I saw a modern road running right through the ramparts, my immediate reaction was one of anger at such callous vandalism. But how wrong my assumptions were, for beneath the road lies an ancient trackway. A careful examination of a map of Woodbury Castle shows quite clearly that the ramparts were built around the road, and not vice versa.

A short distance to the north, this road joins another, and near their intersection is a large tumulus or burial mound known locally as The Beacon. The mound rises high above the surrounding heathland and offers superb panoramic views from its peak. Shaped like an inverted bowl with steeply sloping

Woodbury Beacon, an ancient tumulus where ley lines cross

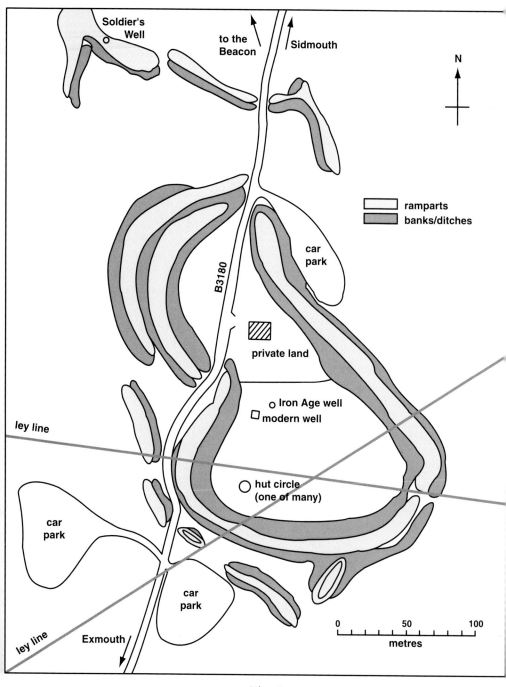

Soldier's Well

to the Beacon

Sidmouth

N

ramparts
banks/ditches

car park

B3180

private land

○ Iron Age well
□ modern well

ley line

○ hut circle
(one of many)

car park

car park

Exmouth

ley line

0   50   100
metres

Fig. 6

40

sides it is topped with pine trees, making it a prominent feature in the landscape. Several other burial mounds of a characteristic Bronze Age circular type have also been found on The Common. The surrounding area has yielded flint tools as well as axe heads made from both polished sandstone and bronze.

Mounds such as The Beacon are referred to by Alfred Watkins in *The Old Straight Track*. They may have names such as 'Tot', 'Toot' or 'Tump', depending on which part of the country they appear, and they are frequently found at the crossing points of ley lines. The Beacon is no exception. Here I dowsed two leys, one running SE-NW and a second, ENE-WSW intersecting at its centre.

Before leaving I made one final check of the perimeter of the castle to see if there were any further ley lines. This proved worthwhile, for there were two: one running NE-SW, and another ESE-WNW. Both crossed in the central enclosure (see fig. 6). This was, I believe, an important area long before the Iron Age ramparts were constructed. Archaeological remains uncovered in the vicinity provide evidence of human presence as far back as Neolithic times (4500-2500 BC), as do the ley lines which only ever aligned places of significance.

By the time I'd started to pack away my equipment, the day was drawing to a close.

I paused for a moment in the cool evening air to glance over to the road where it disappeared into the trees, and thought of all the travellers who over the millennia had passed along it: traders in axes and arrowheads, coming up from Beer Head where the finest flint was to be found; the first herdsmen with their cattle, sheep and goats; the small dark Mediterranean folk, skilled in the working of bronze, who buried their dead beneath the circular mounds known today as barrows; tough Celtic warriors mounted on ponies, fortress builders skilled in the arts of war; Romans who came to conquer, and stayed for three and a half centuries; Saxons, Danes, Normans; and today, one not very significant dowser, overwhelmed by the palpable influence of his historical predecessors.

Dowsing for water

I've already mentioned the close association in most people's minds between dowsing and water finding. Considering that a large proportion (around 65%) of our bodies is made up of water, it is not surprising we have a very close affinity with the substance and that, with instruction and practice, we can find it relatively easily.

This may all sound simple and straightforward, but remember that I previously described water finding as a specialised business. To become accomplished, with repeatedly accurate results, requires a great deal of background knowledge and experience, and for anyone wanting to make an in depth study of this branch of dowsing I strongly recommend George Applegate's excellent book on the subject (see bibliography).

There are many different instruments and methods, but they are all ways of attaining the same end. I have described water finding using a map and pendulum earlier (see page 18), but to begin with, here is an example of how I carry out the job on site.

The ideal place to take water is where two aquifers or underground watercourses cross, known as a blind spring, knot or spiral. This does not necessarily mean that they physically have to meet – their depths could be very different – but that their two energy fields must converge at some point. It is above this convergence on the earth's surface that a spiral can be dowsed. The drilling point is at the exact centre of this spiral.

Before searching there are several criteria to decide upon and programme into the dowser's mind. These come under the headings of: (a) depth, (b) quality and (c) quantity.

(a) Depth: pollution is a sad fact of life nowadays, whether it be from sewage or agricultural chemicals. Even if a site is remote and on a hilltop, I consider it wise to set myself a minimum depth of 9-10 m (30 ft).

(b) Quality: I assess the water quality on a scale of 0–10. Anything over 5 is drinkable, anything below is not. This is a method picked up long ago in *Dowsing: One Man's Way* by

A drilling rig operating in West Cornwall. Water was found soon after this photograph was taken

James Scott Elliot. I like it because it is uncomplicated and never seems to fail.

(c) Quantity: I look for an amount as near to 4500 litres (1000 gallons) an hour as possible, although in practice the amount can fall a little below this figure. Requirements vary according to need, so where a single household is concerned this may not be crucial.

All three assessments are made while standing over the centre of the aquifer – ask for this and you will find it. Once you have done this, lower your rods to your side, then raise them again to the search position. For depth, begin counting slowly and watch for the point where they reach the parallel 'found' position. Note down the figure you have reached. If it helps, try to visualise yourself physically sinking down into the ground until your feet touch that cold water!

For quality, again count slowly, and note the figure when it is reached. When it comes to quantity follow the same procedure once more, this time counting down in litres or gallons per hour.

Two more points worth considering are the distance of the water from where it is needed, and accessibility of the site for a drilling rig, both of which can affect the cost considerably.

A new water supply

Janet was planning to move to a new house being built on the outskirts of a village in mid-Devon. Because of health problems she was unable to drink ordinary tap water, so she rang me to ask if I could go to the site and find a nearby water supply for her. Modern building plots are seldom very big, which means the area to be searched is somewhat restricted, but her need was urgent and I agreed to go and look.

Most of the front of the site was taken up by what was destined to be the driveway, while to the sides and rear was a small garden plot. A walk around the perimeter revealed two aquifers which looked as if they converged beneath the drive. Stepping back so that I was standing sideways on to the boundary I raised the rods in front of me, and began to turn in a circle of search.

When the rods had come together to form a 90° angle, I stopped; then taking a siting through its centre, I began walking forwards. Within a few paces I was directly over the centre of the spring. I circled it and checked each incoming aquifer for depth, quality and quantity, all of which met my requirements: good quality water, well below 9m (30ft), and around 4000 litres (900 gallons) per hour. The spot was clearly pegged, ready for the driller to move in.

*Pengersick Castle, where
thick granite walls hide
many a dark secret*

Spirits

It is common knowledge amongst dowsers that under certain
conditions it is best either to pack up and go home or to divert
your attention to other activities. If, for instance, you are feeling very tired or unwell, or depleted in any way, then stop and
return to the task another day feeling refreshed. This might
cause a slight delay at the time, but in the long term it will pay
dividends in the form of accurate results.

One day in February I was at Pengersick Castle, dowsing and
mapping the site of the original early medieval manor house
which lies beneath woodland to the north-east of the existing
Tudor building. In summer, woodlands can be the most agree-
able of places, with their welcoming shade and tranquillity. But

Trethevy Quoit, near St Cleer, Liskeard, a Neolithic burial chamber built some time between 3500 and 2000 BC, at the crossing point of strong earth energy lines

this was February: water dripped depressingly from the trees as they rocked in a chilling breeze, and a thick misty drizzle drifted in from the sea. I had worked steadily for most of the morning, but now the damp had begun to penetrate my clothing, and even the insides of my normally waterproof walking boots were starting to feel soggy. It was time to move, so I made my way down the hillside to the shelter of the castle.

Whilst drying out in her kitchen, I chatted to Angela Evans about the building and its history. During the conversation the subject of ghosts came up, and Angela told me how The Ghost Club Society, a highly respected psychical research group, had visited Pengersick and conducted several all-night vigils there. The room that interested them most of all was a bedroom on the third storey of the tower, and it was here they claimed to have seen several apparitions: two female figures, a knight and a monk. (The monk had also been seen in other places in the grounds, as well as in a nearby cottage.) I'd previously heard about the reputation of the bedroom, and whenever I'd been in there I'd noticed a distinct coldness in certain areas. Could it be, I pondered, that lines of earth energy crossed at these points, and did they coincide with the places where apparitions had been seen?

First, I must explain the term 'earth energy'. This energy has been known for thousands of years and has been given many different names: Prana, Chi, Wouivre, Munia, to list but a few. Used for healing and immensely powerful, it is the universal life-force that flows within us and all around us, and in its concentrated form it runs in lines above and beneath the earth's surface. These lines can be found by dowsing, and all of the world's great religious structures, from prehistory up until the Reformation, have been carefully laid out on a combined grid of earth energies and lines of underground water.

Pre-Reformation churches, for example, are built on one central east-west earth energy line which is crossed at intervals by others. A line of subterranean water will also be found encircling the altar.

But other phenomena can occur on earth energy lines: they are known to be, particularly at their crossing points, centres of psychic, sometimes poltergeist, activity.

Outside Pengersick the wind still whistled, and the drizzle had turned to a more determined, drenching rain. Any thought of returning to the woodland site was now out of the question.

The haunted bedroom at Pengersick

'Would you mind if I go up to have a look at the haunted room?' I asked Angela.

'Please do!' she replied, 'And if you find anything interesting, let me know.'

I splashed across the courtyard to the great studded oak door and entered the tower. Inside there is a permanent twilight, and such is the thickness of the walls that very little sound from the outside world can filter in. Ahead of me a spiral staircase wound away into the shadows, and as I climbed all I could hear were my own footsteps, coming back to me in a muffled echo from somewhere above.

Passing the entrance to the Drawing Room on my left, I continued upwards to the next floor, where I finally came to a halt in front of a large, substantial-looking door. As the heavy iron latch clicked, the door swung open to reveal the bedroom.

Looking in from the open doorway, the main features on the far wall of the room, from left to right, are a small window, a large finely carved granite fireplace, and a narrow arched entrance leading to a garderobe (a Tudor lavatory, emptied daily by servants).

The wall to the right is lined by two substantial chests and a couple of chairs. To the left of the doorway is a large round-headed mullioned window. Beneath it stands a chest, and two more chairs. But the centre piece of the room, its head against the south wall, is a magnificent four-poster bed, flanked by a table and cupboard. At its foot is another chest, equal in length to the width of the bed.

Several people have told me that they experience great fear whenever they enter this room. This is something I have never felt, but I have noticed that areas within it are extremely cold, even when the weather outside is warm. On this particular day, although I had felt chilled working outside in the wind, once away from it I had been quite comfortable. Here, though, in the bedroom I was starting to feel cold again, and I was glad I'd kept my outside coat on.

Starting on the side of the room opposite the entrance, I began searching for any incoming lines of earth energy, laying a red marker peg on the floor at each point where I got a positive reaction. A complete circuit of the walls finally revealed two lines, crossing just in front of the chest at the foot of the bed. I carefully retraced each line once more to establish the exact point of intersection, and eventually I was standing directly over it with my rods in the found position.

As I stood there, I could feel that the spot was vibrant with energy. I have often experienced this in old churches where energy lines cross. In these places a sensation of warmth can be felt, even in the middle of winter; but here I could only sense a profound coldness, embracing my whole being. I wanted to move, and yet there was something there that urged me to stay. Was it my own curiosity – or was it something else outside me beyond my control? I didn't know; but stay I did, my gaze fixed on the rods in front of me.

The first hint that no ordinary event was about to happen was the appearance of what looked like thin wisps of pure white smoke. They seemed to be emanating from my rods with the dazzling luminosity of ignited magnesium.

On occasions like this I tend to reach out for the rational and the mundane, perhaps as a form of comfort, telling myself that what I'm seeing is not real, just something quite commonplace that can be explained away.

Deliberately shifting my focus of vision, I wanted to eliminate any chance of it being an optical illusion; but illusion it most definitely was not. Even as I watched, the volume of whiteness grew ever more rapidly, and as I glanced down at the floor I realised that it was coming from there and not from my rods.

Up until then the only physical sensation I'd experienced had been coldness, but now other things were beginning to happen: a tingling sensation working its way upwards from my feet was starting to envelop my whole body, and although the room was completely quiet an inner sound, rather like a rushing of wind, was filling my head. Either I was becoming part of the enveloping mist or it was becoming a part of me. I did not know which, but at that moment some instinct of self-preservation from deep inside me shouted 'Stop!' I parted the rods and stepped backwards. My body still tingled, but in that instant the mist had gone and I stood alone in that old, silent room.

Before leaving, I wrote down an account of the whole incident for Angela, who likes to keep a record of all that happens at Pengersick. Late that evening, she rang to tell me she had just spoken to Trevor Kenwood, a leading member of The Ghost Club Society. She had read him the report I'd written for her earlier that day, and had been greeted with such silence that she began to wonder if he had disbelieved the whole episode. However, his reaction had been more of surprise than incredulity, for during one of his early visits to Pengersick he also had gone up to the haunted bedroom, and it was there that he too had witnessed a phenomenon identical to the one I had described that very morning. For a few short moments something or someone had reached out to us from those ancient walls, with their dark brooding history.

Charlotte

The events that took place in rural North Cornwall in the spring and summer of 1844, when a young girl was brutally murdered and her lover arrested, tried and hanged for the crime, should be famous for their very brevity if for no other reason. The murder took place on Sunday 14 April, and by Monday 12 August the remains of the condemned man lay beneath the coalyard in Bodmin gaol. Time, you may think, now to move on, to forget; but the death of Charlotte Dymond has never been forgotten, the story having been passed down through the years from one generation to another. It has been the subject of poetry, prose and film, and now, in true 21st century style, an electronically controlled reconstruction of the trial can be seen at the Shire Hall in Bodmin, the original venue.

Here then is the framework of the story. Charlotte Dymond and Matthew Weeks worked together on the same farm, Penhale, in a remote area bordering the north-eastern sector of Bodmin Moor. They had been lovers for two years, but it is thought that Charlotte had wanted to end the affair. At around four o'clock on Sunday 14 April 1844 they set off together, dressed in their best clothes, through the fields towards Davidstow Common on the moor's edge above the farm.

Late that evening Matthew returned on his own. Charlotte was never seen alive again, but nine days later on Tuesday 23 April her body was discovered, lying beside the stream below Roughtor ford, some four miles from Penhale. Her throat had been cut in what must have been a savage, frenzied attack.

Two days before the discovery of Charlotte's body, Matthew, who by then was being subjected to a barrage of questions from other members of the household as well as from neighbours, had walked out of Penhale, saying that he would return for the evening's milking. He never did, and was later arrested in Plymouth where he had being staying with his sister.

Throughout the trial he maintained his innocence, insisting he had left Charlotte at what was called Down Gate, on the moor's edge, and had gone on to Halworthy in the opposite

THIS
MONUMENT
IS ERECTED by
PUBLIC
SUBSCRIPTION
in
MEMORY
of
CHARLOTTE DYMOND
who was MURDERED here
by
MATTHEW WEEKES
on
SUNDAY
April 14
1844

The memorial to Charlotte Dymond near Roughtor Ford, close to where her body was found. It was erected with money raised by public subscription soon after the murder

direction. Eye witness reports of those who said they'd seen Matthew with Charlotte on the moor lacked consistency, their content changing between the committal hearing and the final trial.

Material and verbal evidence was gathered in a haphazard way by local people and by parish constables who, although obviously dedicated, were by modern standards little better than amateurs. If the trial had been brought before a court today, the prosecution case would have collapsed and Matthew would have walked away a free man. But this was 1844, and the final outcome was death before a leering crowd at the gates of Bodmin gaol.

What is it then about Charlotte Dymond and Matthew Weeks that makes people want to remember their tragedy? It is a question I would never have attempted to answer if I hadn't by chance picked up a book on the subject in my local library. As I turned the pages, I began to feel I was no longer an observer looking in from the outside; slowly, I was being drawn in by a compulsion to be involved, to probe deeper. Instinctively I knew there was something terribly wrong about the case. Linked to this was a strong feeling that help was needed, and whether I liked it or not I had to search for the truth.

What follows is the result of that undertaking. But before beginning, I must say that my choice of book turned out to be particularly fortuitous, for I had happened upon a highly accurate and painstakingly researched work: *The Charlotte Dymond Murder* by Pat Munn. Many of the details I relate here have been gleaned from it, and it is, I believe, essential reading for anyone wanting to make an in-depth study of the case.

Parts of the route taken by Charlotte on that last fateful day were established during the search for her by local people. Rain had left the ground muddy, and she had worn pattens – wooden undershoes set on iron ovals which protected footwear from the damp. These left a distinctive print where the ground was soft.

Prints of a man's boots were also noticed in some of these places, and two of the searchers, William Northam, landlord of the Halworthy Inn, and his neighbour, John Westlake, measured both patten marks and boot prints against a walking stick. They cut notches to mark the appropriate lengths, and later these measurements were compared with those of

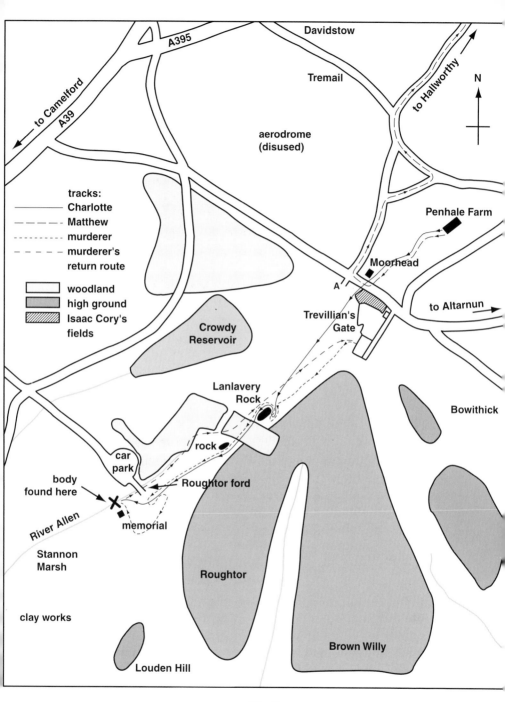

Fig 7

Matthew's boots. They did not match, the prints found on the moor being shorter. This vital piece of evidence came to light at the initial magistrates' hearing, but was shamefully brushed aside at the final trial.

Tracks of any living being can be traced by dowsing (see pages 36-8) and, as long as the dowser is specific about whose footsteps they are searching for and when the person had passed that way, they will stand a good chance of success. If, of course, the person in question was never there at that time, then nothing will be found. The process is no more difficult than dowsing for water; all that's needed is a very clear idea of who or what is being sought.

Charlotte's patten prints had been found between Penhale and the Davidstow–Altarnun road, disappearing where the moorland grass became thicker as she made her way across Davidstow Common towards Lanlavery Rock (locally pronounced 'Lanlary'), a great squat outcrop rising out of the moor 2.5 km distant. Here at the roadside, I reasoned, was a good starting point for my search.

Leaving my car beside a rough track ('A' in fig. 7), not far from the house called Moorhead, I began searching in a south-easterly direction. I followed the edge of the road until I reached the boundary wall of a field (shaded on the map). The question I asked was: 'Can you show me Charlotte's tracks on 14 April 1844?' Not far from the wall my rods swung to the parallel position. This is the way she had passed a hundred and fifty-six years ago, yet from the strength of the reaction it could have been yesterday.

From the wall I retraced my steps, this time searching for Matthew's tracks. There was nothing! I went back to where I'd parked and checked again, this time covering a wider strip of ground. Still nothing… Going out further on to the moor, I repeated the search. Charlotte's path was again crystal clear, but of Matthew there was no trace.

Wherever he was that day, it had not been here, and this conflicted with one of the most damning pieces of evidence at his trial. Isaac Cory, a farmer whose land lay beside the road at

Lanlavery Rock, the meeting place of Charlotte and her killer

nearby Trevillian's Gate, said that when he'd gone there to look at a crop of wheat he'd seen Matthew walking across the moor with a woman wearing a red shawl, about sixty yards from the corner of the field. This, he stated, was at around twenty to five, after he had returned from Davidstow church that Sunday afternoon.

He also admitted he was unable to identify the woman because her face had been hidden beneath an umbrella; but Charlotte had been wearing a red shawl that day.

I had to stop for a moment and think carefully. Matthew had not walked onto the moor from the road, but Charlotte had. There were two sets of tracks which had to be followed: one leading, I knew, to Roughtor Ford and an appointment with sudden death; the other, to who knows where? I made my choice and headed in a south-westerly direction towards Lanlavery Rock. It was a perfect day for being out on the moor, with a clear sky, brilliant sunshine and just enough breeze to make walking comfortable; how different, I thought from that wet misty Sunday all those years ago. All around me was silence, broken only by the bleating of sheep, and somewhere away in the distance the mosquito-like whine of a military helicopter.

Once back on the line of her footsteps, I could follow it quite easily, stopping at intervals to make notes. At around 270 m (300 yd) from the rock, Charlotte turns and looks back in the direction from which she had come. A little further on, and she turns again. She is anxious: either she is making sure that Matthew is not following her or she is wishing he had. Whichever it might be, I feel she is becoming apprehensive: dowsing isn't just about using instruments, it's about feeling, knowing – call it what you will – and this day the intuitive side was very strong.

She approaches Lanlavery Rock from its north-eastern side, walking up the grassy slope. Where the rock is directly to her right, she comes to a halt. Crossing her path at this point are the tracks of a man. It is not Matthew. Both sets of tracks follow each other around in circles. They come together behind the eastern side of the rock, where there is a large outcrop, then continue along the base to a point quite near the centre.

Again they come together, and this is repeated further on. As I write, I have my notebook beside me, and at this point I made the following comment with heavy underlining: 'I think he has her pinned against the rock.' My notes continue: 'Charlotte turns almost on the spot as he confronts her.

This happens four times. I think she is turning, dodging, try-ing to avoid him. When two people talk/embrace and they are on good terms, they rarely dodge around avoiding each other.' I only wish I could have been with William Northam and John Westlake on the day of the search: the footprints beneath Lanlavery Rock would have spoken volumes.

Charlotte climbs the slope between the first outcrop of rocks and the second, followed by whoever is with her, then her tracks veer west-south-west. The man is now alongside, but seven paces away. They pass through what today is a forest plantation, but was then moorland. They are now ten paces apart. As they emerge from this area, they are separated again by a distance of seven paces. Ahead there is another rock outcrop, similar to Lanlavery, but much smaller.

Their footsteps come together at a crevice behind the rock, but once more she moves away, heading off along the hillside towards Roughtor Ford. The man is to her right, five paces away, moving along the top rim of the outcrop.

After walking 90 m (100 yd) they are nine paces apart, and at 270 m (300 yd) the distance has widened to fourteen paces. When they are about 360 m (400 yd) from the rock, Charlotte moves to her right in a semi-circle, intercepting the path of the man. They then move around in circles. It looks very much as if they are conversing. They move on, still in the direction of Roughtor Ford, five paces apart. Charlotte veers away slightly up the slope, increasing the distance between them to ten paces. She again circles to her right, stopping in his tracks.

These traces I picked up of the movements of Charlotte and whoever she was with corroborate well with the evidence of one witness who was on the moor that day. Richard Pethick, a cattle farmer out checking his stock, told of seeing the couple: 'They occasionally stopped and turned about and stood in front of each other, it appeared as if face to face.'

He saw them three times altogether. The third time was around seven o'clock when they were no more than 90 m (100 yd) from the place where the body was found. Apart from her killer, he must have been the last person to have seen Charlotte alive.

One other witness spotted a man and woman together a little earlier in the same area. He was William Gard, a well-known local preacher. He also remarked on them walking first one way and then the other, sometimes stopping, as if in conversation; but they were too far away for him to make any positive identification. His sighting was estimated to have been at around five thirty.

Whatever passed between Charlotte and the man with her along the way between Lanlavery Rock and the descent to Roughtor Ford after they had gone beyond the second outcrop, we do not know, but it is certain that, as they traversed that long

Roughtor Ford

slope of grassland to the stream, they stopped and talked a great deal. If the times mentioned by the two witnesses were correct, then the conversation must have gone on for an hour and a half, if not longer. Whatever they were discussing must have been deeply important to have engaged them for so long.

The last stop they were to make was where the main footpath leading up to Roughtor begins to climb away from the ford. Here, Charlotte turns around to her right, coming face to face with the man, and as before they walk around in circles. The conversation finishes, and she moves away, leaving the ford behind her and heading towards the stream below. When she reaches it, she turns to her left and follows the bank as it curves around in a right-hand bend.

The man turns once more, watching her, I think, before moving off in the direction from which they had come. But it is not long before his track veers to the right; he is making a long, slow detour back towards Charlotte. He passes over marshy ground and along a course which takes him just to the right of where the memorial to her now stands. I wonder if she was aware of his approach – my feeling is that she was not. As he attacks, she spins rapidly around in an anti-clockwise direction, and she falls to the ground.

So ends the life of Charlotte Dymond, a pathetically short existence of only eighteen years.

She was not murdered by Matthew Weeks, of that I am convinced. Time and again I have checked for any sign of his tracks along the course of her final walk that Sunday evening. They are nowhere to be found – but there is ample evidence of someone else's presence: that of her killer. And his identity? We can never be absolutely sure. Here is the remaining evidence I've gathered from my dowsing research…

I've returned to the spot where Charlotte's tracks first met those of the man, beside Lanlavery Rock, and I have gone back over his footsteps. They come from a gateway leading into a field at Trevillian's Gate.

To confirm I had not been mistaken, I covered the ground once more, ending up in exactly the same place (the gate in 1844 was considerably narrower than the galvanised steel model which now occupies the spot).

From the site of the murder, I have followed the man's return journey along the course of the stream where his progress was hidden by a high bank rising to the south-east, past the turf-pit where he'd secreted some of the clothes taken from the body (probably having already washed the blood from them), and on into an area now filled with trees. Where his tracks re-emerged onto open ground I was surprised to find myself no more than 13.5 m (15 yd) from the path he and Charlotte had taken earlier that evening.

His path now takes him past Lanlavery Rock, keeping it around 180 m (200 yd) to his right; then slowly, he begins to change direction, heading further to the east. Ahead of me there is a gateway – the same one from which he had emerged earlier on the way to his meeting with Charlotte. When he is some 140 m (150 yd) from it, he stops and turns to face the direction from which he has come. Now Charlotte is no more, and he must take care not to be seen. He turns and, approaching the gate from the left-hand side, slips quietly through, out of sight and out of mind.

And then there is Matthew. Where is he while the story is unfolding? To find out I had to return to the area around Moorhead which is where he said he last saw Charlotte. Together with its surrounding land the house stands in an area which in 1844 was moorland. The path from Penhale came out from the corner of a field below, at a place then known as Downgate. It would have led out onto the Camelford–Altarnun road from what is now the entrance to Moorhead. A search for any traces of Matthew along the moorland side of the road had produced no results. Perhaps, I reasoned, it would be worth crossing over and checking beside the stone hedge forming the Moorhead boundary.

The next available day, a stiff breeze gusted across Davidstow Common and a heavily overcast sky threatened rain. As I drove along past the abandoned World War II aerodrome, I was glad that this time I would not be venturing out onto the open moor, a place where even the most promising of weather can prove unpredictable.

Parking in the same spot I'd used on my first visit, I once again picked up Charlotte's footsteps across the road from Moorhead, this time following them back in the direction from which she had come.

I searched on either side of where she had walked for any sign of Matthew, and there to her right, emerging from what is now a gateway, I found his tracks. Like Charlotte's, they were as clear and precise as if they had been left the previous day. This is the point at which the couple went their separate ways: she across the road and onto the moor, and he to the right, following the line of the present wall.

A little way down the road and his track turns right down a turning marked Tremail. He keeps to the right-hand edge of the road, past where there is now a cattle grid, then on over the brow of the hill. He pauses in a gateway on the right-hand side, and crosses over to the left where he remains until reaching a turning marked St Clether. Here he turns right, keeping very close to the right-hand corner.

After about half a mile, he comes to a T-junction. Will he, I wonder, turn right onto a road which would eventually bring him back to Penhale? I travel a short way in this direction, and check for signs of him in two separate places. There is nothing. Back at the T-junction, I take the left-hand turn and soon pick up his path again. After almost another half mile, he makes a right turn, and then at the bottom of a hill, right again, passing a farm called Trewinnow.

By now I am almost certain his destination is Halworthy, but one lesson I have learned with dowsing is never take anything for granted: the unexpected is always lurking behind the next corner, waiting to make nonsense of any cherished preconceptions we may be nurturing. It is better by far to erase them from the mind, and even to forget about logic and reasoning, the only faculty to be brought into play being pure intuition.

The road narrows and, after descending a hill lined with high hedges, crosses over the River Inney. Matthew crossed this bridge too, his path clear as ever. On he goes, following the steep winding road on the other side. Where it starts to level out, I follow his footsteps over the brow onto the ridge above. Here his course begins to meander. He is tired from the walk and, I think, dejected at having lost Charlotte, his love for the last two years.

A short distance down the road is Halworthy, now his undoubted destination. Why then did he go there?

He had to go somewhere; anywhere would be better at this moment than Penhale, where his young man's pride would be wounded when the news of his rejection by Charlotte became common knowledge. Ironically, had he swallowed this pride and returned from Downgate as soon as she had left him, the whole outcome of the story would have been so different: poor tragic Matthew, the victim of fickle circumstance and youthful vanity…

History books are filled with the exploits of the wealthy and the mighty, their features recorded for posterity by the world's greatest artists and in latter years by photographers. But what of the ordinary people, the Matthews and the Charlottes of this world? We may know something of their lives, but their faces seem destined to remain an enigma.

Some years ago, I discovered that if I sat alone with a pencil and paper in front of me sometimes faces would begin to take shape. I describe it in that way because it never feels as if it is me doing the drawing. My own attempts at any sort of artwork in the past have been confined to badly executed caricatures of colleagues, borne for the most part with long-suffering good humour.

Who these faces are often remains a mystery, coming as they do unannounced, their only remarkable quality being the individuality of their features which are completely unfamiliar to my conscious mind. Occasionally I treat it rather like a dowsing exercise, asking a question and waiting for an answer which, if it is there, will come to me in the form of a picture.

I once lived in a very old cob-walled cottage deep in the Devonshire countryside. I never actually saw any presences there, although my son tells me he did; but I could, with some kind of inner sense, 'feel' they were around. On two separate occasions, two very contrasting, very memorable faces took shape, the style of each image being entirely different. I knew with certainty that at some time in the past they had both lived in the cottage.

To my knowledge, no likeness of Charlotte Dymond was ever made during her lifetime. But I was still curious about what she looked like.

One evening, alone in my study and with this question in mind, I turned away from my writing and sat with notepad and pencil, waiting. After what seemed a very long pause in which nothing happened, the pencil started to move with ever increasing speed.

Within a few minutes, it had slowed and came to a halt. From the paper a face looked back at me. On the following page you will find that image.

As a final word for those of you who would like to visit the area where the Charlotte Dymond murder took place, I must emphasise that Penhale Farm, Moorhead and the land surrounding them are all private property. There is no public right of way through them. Please remember this and respect the rights of the owners. Access to the moor is not restricted, but it is a livestock grazing area, so keep dogs under control and take your litter home. Bodmin Moor is a wild and beautiful place. I hope it will give you as much pleasure as it always gives me.

Shadows of a saint – dowsing a sacred well

Early in the fifth century, when the last of the Roman legions departed from Britain to defend the troubled borders of a crumbling empire, over 360 years of Roman rule came to an end, leaving the province undefended. To the east the coastline lay open to attack from Saxon, Angle and Jute raiders, but in the far west life continued much as it always had done, with contact being maintained between the lands of what is now known as the Celtic Arc.

At this time a group of voyagers from Wales and Ireland began arriving in Cornwall, landing mainly in the Hayle and Camel estuaries. These were the 'Saints' who were to be immortalised in many Cornish place names; not saints in the canonical sense, but so-called because of their exceptional ability to teach and spread 'the word'. Schooled in the monastic traditions of the Celtic church, the evangelists brought with them their own individualistic brand of Christianity.

One of their number, a Welshman named Clether, or in Latin Clederus, settled in the valley of the River Inney where the water flows down from Bodmin Moor. (Clether is said to have been one of twenty-four children of Brychan, a tribal leader. Each of the twelve boys and twelve girls were destined to become saints.) Here, beneath craggy outcrops lining the valley's edge and close by a spring, he built an oratory.

My first visit to St Clether's valley was so many years ago that it is difficult to pinpoint an exact time, but impressions of the day remain indelibly on my mind: young ravens – sunlight mirrored on new plumage – tumbling in first clumsy flight over their rocky nest-site; the white flowers and feathery leaves of pignut plants growing in a scatter over the turf; a profusion of blackthorn bramble and hazel; the lush greenness of bracken fronds; and the golden blossom of gorse filling the air with its sweet almond scent.

Above it all were rocks – massive, weathered rocks, jutting out from the steep hillside, their coat of lichen glowing white in the summer light; and beneath them, a path leading down to the

St Clether's Well hides behind the chapel. Here we can see the well building and the east wall of the chapel. The altar is just inside the window. Water is supposed to flow from the well through a channel behind the altar

valley where the River Inney winds its way through verdant beds of rushes.

As it is approached from the footpath, the chapel only comes into view when you are almost upon it. Half hidden by trees and tucked in beneath the hillside, it is a secret, secluded place, ideally suited to the solitary lifestyle that Clether would have led.

Water has always been of great importance to mankind as a vital life-sustaining substance, but over the millennia it also assumed a spiritual significance. To toss a coin in a fountain or a well and to make a wish is a custom with ancient origins, and the practice of leaving offerings of weapons, jewellery and other precious objects in these places can be traced back as far as the

Middle Bronze Age (around 1500 BC). And at one time it was believed that places where water came out of the ground were contact points with the underworld – the dwelling place of the gods – from which life emerged and disappeared.

Celtic Christians carried on the tradition of venerating wells and springs, and St Clether was no exception. Some waters were known to possess the power to heal, and there were wells that gained a reputation for curing specific complaints. In certain cases this could possibly have been due to the mineral content of the water, but in others there could be no easy explanation.

The spring feeding St Clether's well emerges from the ground to the north-east of the chapel. It runs first into a stone basin housed within the small well building, then flows through a notch cut in the basin's rim, down a channel that was laid beneath the east wall of the chapel, and behind the altar. Finally it spills out into a second basin built into the south-east wall.

Straying water

Problems arising from this watercourse led to some recent dowsing visits to St Clether. The well has always been noted for its unfailing supply of water, but increasingly during the summer months it has no longer spilled out over the notch in the first basin and along its channel behind the altar. This decline in level was first observed in the arid summer of 1976, and the situation has continued to worsen. However, I did notice that a good flow emerged from beneath the hedge surrounding the lower side of the ground on which the building stands, so the water was obviously escaping somewhere.

After finding the place (A in fig. 9) where the aquifer emerges from the hillside and enters the rear north-east corner of the well building, I walked around to the notch at the front of the basin (B), and looked in at the pool of water. Although crystal clear, it was still – too still. If water is flowing into, and out of, a well basin, some movement, however slight, can always be detected either in vegetation growing around the rim or in minute particles suspended below the surface. But here there was nothing.

I searched with my rods for any signs of a flow along the western wall. Not only did I detect it emerging from beneath this wall, I could hear the distinct gurgle of running water close to the surface (C). Following it towards the chapel, I found the spot where it disappeared beneath the building (D). Inside, it ran beneath the floor to the south wall, then out again on the lower side, aligning exactly with the point beneath the hedge where it had already been noticed coming to the surface.

A close examination of the interior walls at the places where the water entered and left the building revealed signs of damp having risen and soaked deep into the stonework. Left unchecked this will cause severe damage, especially in frosty conditions.

So it would seem the problem originates from where the spring should enter the well basin. Instead, it is flowing either around or beneath it. Only by digging will the full extent of the required corrective work be revealed, but I hope that soon the sound of holy well water will once again be heard, summer and winter, making its way through the chapel.

An unwritten history

Of the two buildings now seen in the little hollowed-out field (known as Chapel Park) certain historical facts are known. In their original form they both pre-dated the Norman church standing 400 metres further down the valley. By the fifteenth century they were in such a bad state of repair that they had to be rebuilt. Later they were left to deteriorate again so that by the nineteenth century the roofs and much of the walls had fallen in, thorns and brambles had taken root among the masonry, and the whole area had become an inaccessible bog.

Luckily help was at hand in the form of the Reverend Sabine Baring-Gould, rector of Lewtrenchard and novelist, antiquary, and writer of such well-known hymns as 'Onward Christian Soldiers'.

Together with the Reverend A H Malan, the vicar of Altarnun, and moral and financial assistance from the land-owner Mr T Spry of Witherdon, a remarkably sympathetic and careful

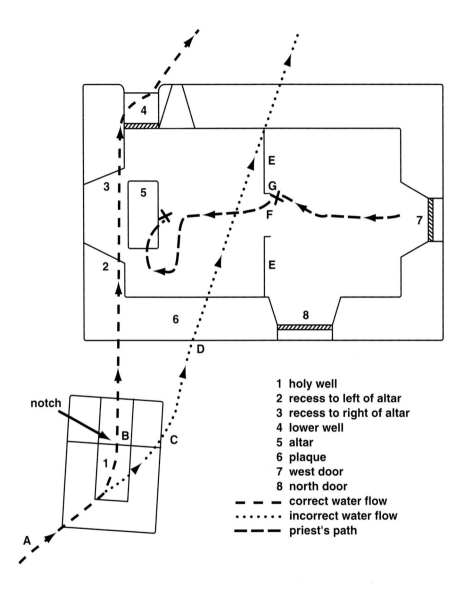

1 holy well
2 recess to left of altar
3 recess to right of altar
4 lower well
5 altar
6 plaque
7 west door
8 north door
 — — — correct water flow
 .... incorrect water flow
 — — priest's path

Fig. 9

restoration was achieved: quite a rarity in an age not renowned for its sensitivity in these areas.

Although the original plan was to renovate only the well, work was extended to include the chapel, culminating in the reconstruction of both buildings. The well house differs from the original in that, instead of a domed roof, it now has a 'ridge and roll' type similar to those found at other Cornish wells.

Re-dedication took place in 1900, and since then little has altered. The chapel was re-roofed and repointed in the early 1990s, and a few years later the well roof was realigned and re-bedded, and its walls were repointed.

When compared with the surrounding area, Chapel Park is an obvious anomaly, being a level rectangle surrounded by steep rough ground. The central placement of the fifteenth-century buildings within its bounds would suggest it was excavated at the same time as their rebuilding programme took place.

These, then, are the supposed facts, but as I studied them I became increasingly aware of gaps in our knowledge of St Clether's well and its history. With each fact there seemed to be an accompanying question: Was the present chapel preceded by an earlier one on the same site? Had the altar, as Baring-Gould assumed, always been in the same place, or had it ever been moved? If the well and chapel were completely rebuilt in the fif-teenth century on newly excavated ground, were they on the site of Clether's original oratory, or was that somewhere else? If the oratory was elsewhere, then was there another, much older pathway in?

There was only one way to find answers to these questions, and that was by dowsing. Not only are springs issuing from the ground a regular feature of north Cornwall: equally common, especially in moorland areas, can be the water that feeds them, falling in copious quantities from the sky. It was on just such a rain-drenched day that I returned to St Clether's well.

Opposite: St Clether's well. Beneath its weathered stones the water emerges from the hillside

Vanda Inman, who looks after the well and its chapel

I was accompanied by Vanda Inman, whose family have owned Well Park for three generations. Since becoming the owner, she has taken on the responsibilities of tending it in much the same way as it would have been done in the past by 'Well Guardians', a group of dedicated women who were so much a feature of these places during the nineteenth century.

Vanda has a deep love for the well and chapel, and the surrounding valley, so much so that it has become a major part of her life. It has also become the focal point of ongoing study, and she is the author of two guide books: one on the well, and the other about St Clether parish church (see page 79). Like me, she was anxious to seek answers to a great many questions.

While the rain tumbled down outside, I stood in the twilight of the chapel, facing the massive granite altar beneath the east window. It is a small, bare building, the only other furnishings being two benches and a chair – somehow befitting the simple requirements and meagre lifestyle of a Celtic saint.

'Was there,' I asked, 'another building on this site before the fifteenth century – and, if there was, can I be shown the position of the walls?' The question was set in my mind, and I moved forwards, my rods in the search position. As I passed the north door on my left-hand side, I could feel the rods starting to move inwards. A little further on, and they were parallel with each other. I was over a wall (E). Further inspection revealed a door at its centre (F), which was aligned with the present west door and of a similar width.

Next, I needed to know the age of this wall. Using dowsing techniques explained on page 9, I discovered that it had been constructed in the eighth century (the north, east and south walls of the much earlier building lay directly beneath their fifteenth-century counterparts). Its dimensions were 3.5 x 5.2 m (11 x 17 ft), making it approximately half the size of the present building. I searched the area within the walls to see if there had been any other structure on the site, pre-dating it. There was nothing.

Stepping into the footsteps of someone from the past can often reveal useful information (see page 36). Standing just inside the west door (see fig. 9, location 7), I asked to follow the footsteps of the priest or monk as he entered the eighth-century chapel. As I approached the doorway, I was led to the right-hand door post where I stopped with my rods crossed. Question and answer revealed this to be the position of the stoup, or basin, built into the wall to hold holy water.

The priest continued down the centre of the building, turning left just before the altar, and then right, into the corner between the north and east walls.

Then something strange happened. His path now headed towards a spot directly in front of the centre of the altar, where he would have stood during a service; but instead of passing around the corner of the altar to reach this point, he walked 'right through'. Any such exercise today would result in severe bruising from contact with a thick lump of granite. There was, of course, a simple explanation: the altar in the eighth century stood about 28 cm (11 in) back from the position it occupies today. I was able to confirm this by dowsing for its exact original position.

An additional piece of evidence was discovered when we examined the back of the slab: the sides and front of the stone were dressed and smooth; the rear was roughly finished and was not intended to be seen – it must have been slotted into the east wall beneath the window. I believe that if Sabine Baring-Gould had been a dowser, he would not have been so adamant in his statement that the altar had never been moved!

There are two recesses built into the east wall of the chapel: one is to the left of the altar, put there, it is believed, as an access point to the water channel, perhaps for keeping it clear; the other lies to the altar's right-hand rear side (see fig. 9). It is thought this second recess played a major part in the devotional life of the chapel, for it is here that the bones – the 'relics' – of St Clether would have been placed on special occasions, such as pilgrimages, or services of healing. The water would then run over the bones on its way to the lower well, where it would have been drunk. There was a strong belief, inherited from pre-Christian days, that relics enhanced the healing qualities of water.

An examination of the interior of the recesses revealed the granite channel designed to carry water from the top to the bottom well, concealed for most of its course beneath the east wall. A check for the year of their installation revealed that they had been there since 1340, but they superseded an earlier water course.

The altar is far older than anything else in the building. It was made around AD 380. Although it is reputed to have been used by St Clether, its age poses a conundrum. If he and his fellow saints arrived in the fifth century, the altar predates their arrival by at least fifty years. Either he came to Cornwall considerably earlier than previously thought, or the altar was already in use somewhere in the vicinity before his time.

Here, then, is a summary of all the evidence I gathered with Vanda Inman:

The chapel standing today dates from the fifteenth century.

Part of it was built on, or incorporated into, an earlier eighth-century building through which ran a watercourse connecting both wells. This meant that only a part of Well Park was excavated and levelled in the fifteenth century, some of the work having already been carried out 700 years previously.

Before 1340 water ran through the eastern end of the chapel, directly beneath the altar, but in this year alterations were made: a more sophisticated system of channels was installed within, rather than in front of, the east wall.

During the course of this work, the altar was moved 28 cm (11 in) back from the wall, and a window sill was inserted.

The altar, made in 380, is on a site where no building existed until the eighth century. It must have been brought here from somewhere else.

Healing waters

Outside the sky still looked threateningly grey, but for a while the rain abated. We had eaten our sandwiches sitting on a chapel bench, watched by a short-tailed vole who had emerged from a recess beside the altar to scurry fearlessly around the floor searching for crumbs. Leaving him to finish his lunch, we ventured outside to look at the well.

In addition to the water emerging from the ground in the form of a spring, holy wells usually have deep aquifers beneath them. Dowsing over St Clether's well, two of these will be found, crossing directly below the centre of the well-house (see fig. 11).

The first runs under the chapel, flowing in an arc around the front of the altar at a depth of 26 m (86 ft). Earth energy is also found here, with two lines crossing in the same place as the aquifers. This combination of water and energy can be felt quite distinctly by a dowser when he or she puts their hand into the entrance of a holy well, just as it can be detected in churches

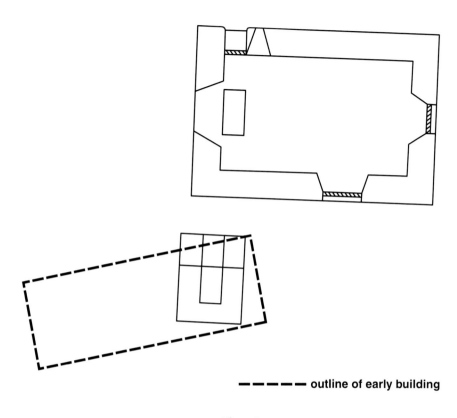

- - - - - outline of early building

Fig. 10

built before the Reformation. It is the reason why being in, or close to, such places is so often described as 'spiritually uplifting'.

Water absorbs emanations as well, thereby becoming holy water and taking on the power to heal. So, there is a very definite purpose in retaining water in a basin above the junction of lines, for it is here it can attain maximum potency. Surrounding junctions are spirals of energy, pulsating out from their centre, like ripples from a pool when a stone has been thrown in.

As I stood in front of the well, I wondered how this place would have looked in St Clether's time. If he was here in the fifth century, there were likely to be traces of a building nearby.

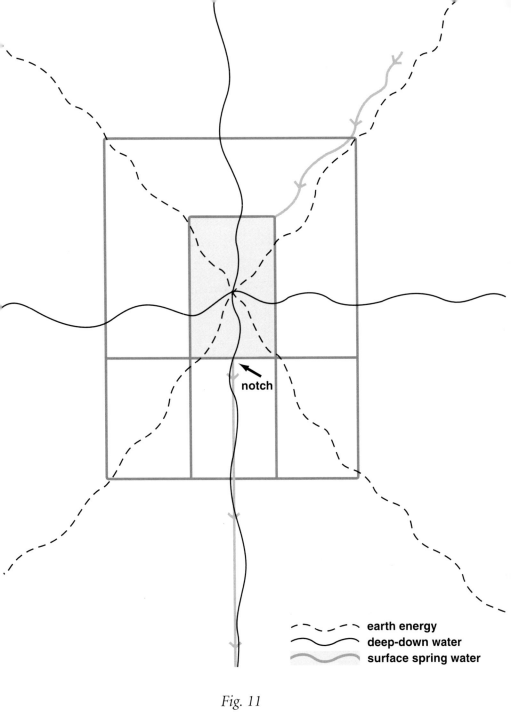

notch

earth energy
deep-down water
surface spring water

Fig. 11

Craggy outcrops look down on St Clether's Well and Chapel

Picking a random date I asked: 'Was there a building here in AD 450?' The response was positive. I searched with my L rods for traces of walls of that date. Over the area covered by the present well, I picked up the outline of one, its alignment entirely different from that of the structure standing there today.

Tracing the entire outline was not easy, the slope being steep and slippery and covered in thick undergrowth. The approximate dimensions were 2.7 x 7.3 m (9 x 24 ft), and part of it stood over the well. The most striking feature was that this building pointed almost due east, and was more accurately orientated than the fifteenth-century chapel beside it.

Taking into account the date, the orientation and the positioning over the well, I believe this has every likelihood of being the original oratory. Its high positioning would have been sensible, as the level ground now occupied by the existing chapel would in 450 have been a marshy hillside, the water from the spring spilling out over it.

When, I wondered, had this building been erected, and how long had it stood here – and was this the original home of the granite altar? To the first question the response was 360; to the second, 340 years; and to the third, 'yes'. So building and altar both pre-date St Clether's supposed arrival date. Whether Christian or Pagan, here was a very ancient place of worship, the sacred spring flowing out from beneath its walls.

Later in the afternoon, slithering around on a treacherous hillside, we discovered the faint remains of a redundant pathway leading down to the original oratory site. Its course up the valley followed the line of rocky outcrops, running along at their base on dry ground: a logical route for travellers in the days when most valleys were impassable marshy forest.

We followed it as far as we could, until halted by an impenetrable thicket of blackthorn. As if colluding with this latest frustration, the drizzle that had been falling for most of the afternoon turned into a determined downpour. Even dowsers can sometimes be defeated by too much water. It was time to go home.

There is much still to be done at St Clether's well: more research, more dowsing – both of which will, I hope, throw a few beams of much needed light on the Dark Ages, a period so lacking in written history.

Bibliography and addresses

Applegate, George   *The Complete Guide to Dowsing* (Element, 1997)

Broadhurst, Paul   *Secret Shrines* (Pendragon Press, 1988)

Evans, Angela   *Pengersick Castle, A Brief History* (Available at Pengersick Castle, Praa Sands, Penzance, Cornwall.)

Inman, Vanda   *Legacy of a Cornish Saint – a guide to St Clether Church and Holy Well*
Legacy of a Cornish Saint – a guide to St Clether Chapel and Holy Well
(Both are available at the Church and at the Holy Well.)

Kenward, Trevor & Snow, Robert *The Ghosts, Hauntings, Myths and Legends of Pengersick Castle, Praa Sands, Cornwall* (KT Kenward and RM Snow, Dorset)

Lonegren, Sig *Spiritual Dowsing* (Gothic Image Publications, 1991)

Miller, Hamish & Broadhurst, Paul *The Sun and the Serpent* (Pendragon Press, 1989)

Munn, Pat *The Charlotte Dymond Murder, Cornwall 1844* (Bodmin Books, 1978)

Scott Elliott, James *Dowsing: One Man's Way* (The British Society of Dowsers, 1990)

Thurnell-Read, Jane *Geopathic Stress – How Earth Energies Affect our Lives* (Element, 1996)

Underwood, Guy *The Pattern of the Past* (Abacus, 1974)

Watkins, Alfred *The Old Straight Track* (Abacus, 1990)

For further information on dowsing:
The British Society of Dowsers
Sycamore Barn
Hastingleigh
Ashford
Kent
TN25 5HW
Tel: (01233) 750253   E-mail: bsd@dowsers.demon.co.uk